Sex Positions

The Sex Bucket List

For Divorced Women

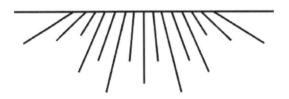

100 Sexy Positions and Naughty Challenges

Madison West

The Sex Bucket List Challenge
for Divorced Women

How long has it been since you've been with a new man?

Just the thought of kissing new lips is a bit nerve-wracking, right?

No worries. The Sex Bucket List is here to revive your sexy side, awaken your confidence, and turn you into a dating queen...both in the bedroom and out.

Ready to Get Naughty?

There are 100 Sex Bucket List Challenges in Total...

To play, divorced chicks will wipe their sexual slate totally clean and start from the very beginning. We're talking **Virgin Territory!**

You'll make your way through this dirty list, choosing kinky positions and wild fantasies to knock off your Sex Bucket List as a newly single woman.

It's time to rediscover what you like and how you like it.

Challenge that teach you sex tips, seductive tricks, and how to make men beg for your attention - by the end of this list, you'll be the best version of yourself, both in the bedroom and out.

Plus, you've never cum this much in your life. I guarantee it....

You have full permission....no, I order you...to get as dirty and freaky as you possibly can.

Are you ready?

Table of Dirty Contents

The Sex Bucket List Rules

Every game has rules. These rules are just a bit more... kinky.

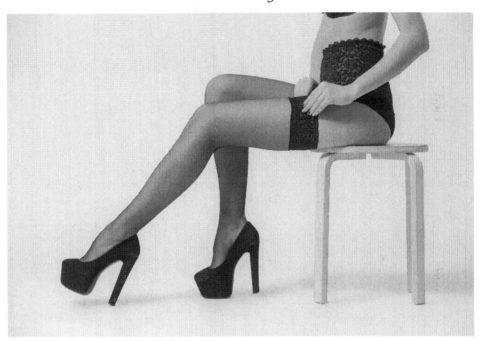

Rule 1: Welcome Back to Virginity

••

Enjoy it. It won't last long...

For all intents and purposes, every divorced chick embarking on The Sex Bucket List is now a virgin again! That's right, you are brand new to the sex game!

✓ You've never been touched before.

✓ You've never given oral.

✓ You've never stuck your tongue down a stranger's throat.

...you get the picture.
That means, you cannot go through the list crossing off dirty things that you've already done...because remember, you're officially a virgin (again).

Rule 2: Let your Sex Drive Choose

••••••••••••••••••••••••••••••••••

When a naughty opportunity presents itself or you get a certain urge to play out a fantasy – go for it.

Just like foreplay, you don't have to go through this sex bucket list in any particular order.

Start with whatever turns you on in the moment.

Rule 3: Push your Limits

• •

Sexual pleasure lies right outside of your erotic comfort zone. You're going to need an open mind and a willingness to be vulnerable.

Of course, the idea of going to a sex club is nerve-racking...but it's also fucking awesome.

Start slow and work your way up to the challenges that push you the most.

Rule 4: Never Fake an Orgasm

· ·

Faking an orgasm isn't doing anyone any favors. You aren't getting off and he isn't learning. You don't owe him an orgasm!

When you don't cum, the guys who are worth your time start to view you as a challenge. You become the sexual puzzle they want to solve.

And when he finally does make you orgasm after a few failed attempts, it will be like he won the god damn lottery. It's often a bonding experience.

There's no shame in not cumming with a stranger. Hell, with a guy that you're dating, it can take a few sessions to get on the same page. Just relax and let it happen.

If you need to reassure him, tell him that it just takes you time to get comfortable with him. Guys like a challenge.

Rule 5: Don't Pretend to be a Slut

• •

And don't pretend to be a pro.

If your last marriage was sexless and this list makes you a little nervous- that's okay! Innocence is sexy. And this is the last time you'll be innocent. So play it up!

If your last marriage was kinky and dirty as can be, more power to you! Just be sure not to make your new partner feel inadequate.

Your sex life is driving at a totally different speed this time. Make it natural.

Laugh when things feel awkward. Be honest if you don't know what you're doing.

Communicate when teaching your partner how to make you cum.

This sexual adventure is all about learning and discovering; not about being a porn star.

No pressure! Just fun!

Rule 5: Wait on Challenges Marked with "xxx"

●●●●●●●●●●●●●●●●●●●●●●●●●●●●●●●●●●●

When you see a **"xxx"** next to a Bucket List Challenge, this means that there must be **at least 1 hour between** the completion of one sex challenge and the choosing of the next.

This, my young friends, is called *Delayed Sexual Gratification.*

Some of these challenges are meant to leave you thirsty for more. You are meant to replay that hot make out session over and over in your head while at work. And you're supposed to leave your crush absolutely begging for another taste.

So, practice a little self-control...it will make your orgasms (and sex appeal) 10x as strong.

Rule 6: Easy Out

•••••••••••••••••••••••••••••••••

If there is a challenge that you absolutely are not into...like "Have a Threesome"– you can skip it...but with a catch.

You are allowed to pass on ONLY 3 of the Bucket List Challenges. Every time your pass on a challenge, you must combine two challenges to create one new challenge.

For example;
- ✓ **Have a threesome**
- ✓ **Hook up with your ex-boyfriend**
- ✓ **Watch porn**

New challenges could be...
- ✓ **Watch porn with your ex-boyfriend**

See what we did there?

You must complete a total of 100 challenges by the end of the list. No cheating & no skipping!

Rule 7: Approach each Challenge with Confidence

••••••••••••••••••••••••••••••••

"Confidence is the sexiest thing a woman can have".

You hear this phrase all the fucking time because it's fucking true.

Guess what? You don't have to look like an Instagram model to have your phone blowing up with male admirers.

And men don't have to be a 6'4, 195lbs to have women fantasizing about them at night.

Play by these rules of thumb, and you can have any man you want:

✓ Confidence is so sexy.

✓ Taking initiative is hot.

✓ And knowing what you want is a huge turn on.

The Sex Bucket List Challenge is here to push that confidence and give you plenty of opportunities to practice it.

This book is the best wing man you've ever had.

Rule 8: Recognize your Sexual Power

• •

Now that you're a single lady, you really have the space to explore who you are.

More specifically, you have the space to explore your sexuality, its power and how that power plays a role in your life.

Sexuality is more than your body and more than your worth. Sexuality comes from your mind, your soul, and your spirit.

How to Keep Track & Keep Pace

Dating post-divorce can be exciting and intimidating at the same time. To get back into the dating game and discover who you are as a single woman, you'll need to dedicate yourself physical and mentally to your mission.

You are now a student of sex and you'll need to take notes on your sexual research.

The best way to **keep track** of your progress through the Sex Bucket List Challenge is with 2 colored pens and a notebook.

When you finish a naughty task, write it down and number it.

Keep pace by doing, **at the very least,** 4 **challenges per week**.

Once you've written 100 challenges down in your notebook, you'll have transformed yourself from the woman who you used to be to the woman who you want to be.

Don't lose the momentum, babe!

The Sex Bucket List Pact

Your first challenge starts now.

Take your top off, stand in front of the mirror and say, "I'm the hottest that I've ever been. My tits are perfect, my ass is beautiful, and my mind is dirty. I'm ready to play".

Say it one more time.

Was that weird? Good.

Things are about to get a whole lot weirder.

Remember, you don't have to go in order. Let your libido do the picking...

Chapter 1: Pick your Prey

You've been having sex with the same partner night after night for who knows how long! It's time to switch it up.

Now that your sexual power is taking form, use it like a bullet. Set your eyes on a target and hunt him down.

Here is a simple list of every sexual partner you should cross off during singledom. Use these guys to help you complete The Sex Bucket List as you go along! You can cross your prey off the list once you've successfully shared a dirty challenge...

1. Your High School Crush

We all have an old flame or a lingering crush from high school, that given the chance, we would totally bang. Now is that chance!

Find your lover boy on Facebook, social media, or at the bar where he usually hangs out, confirm that he's not married (you're no homewrecker), and then put the moves on him! Odds are, he's been thinking about you, too...that's the way these things usually work.

2. Your Cute Neighbor

Whether it's the newly divorced dad down the street, the guy you've had a crush on for years or the hottie in your new building– this close proximity makes for the perfect late-night booty call.

Play up the "newly single woman in distress role" and ask him to come fix your sink...while you're not wearing a bra (of course).

3. Your Coworker

Listen, you've been off-limits to all the men at work while you were married...but that doesn't mean that your male coworkers haven't been fantasizing about you the whole time. And now that you're single, you are a bright red glowing dot on their radar. The chase is on!

You can finally flirt back and even invite one for drinks...

4. An Older Man

Let an older man show you how it's done! It's time that you let someone else take the reins and show you what you've been missing. Older men are usually way kinkier than you and will be thrilled to have a hot piece of ass at their fingertips.

Ps. YOU are the hot piece of ass.

5. A Younger Man

Oh, Hello Ms. Robinson. You are now the sexy MILF (even if you don't have kids) that every young guy has fantasized about. Take charge and teach this younger guy exactly how you like it while you enjoy his tight young body and insatiable sexual appetite.

6. A Bartender

Now that you have a little more free time on your hands, you might find yourself going out more often with your single girlfriends. Once you start frequenting the same bar...you're going to develop a crush on the local bartender. It's just science: drinks + hot man serving you drinks who knows you by name= crush.

Hang out until late, ask him when he gets off his shift, and make it known that you are DTF.

7. Stranger from the Bar

Guess what! Now you can finally take a man home from a bar for some carnal, no-strings attached sex. That's right. See him, eye-fuck him, have him buy you a drink and then take him home for a good ol' one-night stand.

Pro Tip: If you live alone, always opt for these strangers come to come home with you. Being in your own territory gives you more power and safety...and less of a chance of winding up in some psycho's sex dungeon.

8. That Guy on Vacation

Babe, you deserve to treat yourself to a 'Restart Weekend'! Go on a little vacay. Whether you're taking a luxury cruise down the Panama Canal, flying to Mexico for a cheap AirBnb weekend or just driving to another city to stay with a girlfriend for the weekend – set your sights on finding an out-of-town fling!

9. The Guy from the Gym

If you haven't already, get your ass back in the gym after your divorce. I'm not talking about 5x a week...I'm talking about at least 2x per week to get back in touch with your body and remember what it feels like to have guys check out your ass (because they will).

Keep this routine up and start making flirty eyes at the men whom you find attractive. Keep the signals open that you're approachable, put yourself at the water fountain the same time as your target, and let those workout hormones take their course.

10. A Man from Another Country

Pick a guy with a sexy accent and a foreign passport for one night of fun.

Bonus points if he doesn't even speak the same language!

Extra bonus points if he's only in town for the weekend! Let this guy be the one you fantasize about for years to come....

11. An Ex-boyfriend

Was there a guy you dated before you got married? Have you ever wondered what it would be like to give him another chance? In order to move on from your past, you've got to resolve everything...and everyone.

Start chatting up that old lover and get those years of pent up sexual energy out! It will either dissolve the thought of him completely, allowing you to get rid of that "What if" in your head. Or it might turn into something. There's only one way to find out...

12. Tinder Boy

Or Bumble Boy. Or Coffee Meets Bagel Boy. Whatever you dating app suits your personality, go for it girl! The world of online dating is fun and fruitful. Yes, these apps are full of shallow pricks...but there are also some really good guys that are worth your time.

13. Another Woman

For now, just start with the softcore stuff. Keep your eye out for a woman who turns you on. Maybe this is a girl at the bar, maybe a girl at work, or even a girl you've found on Tinder. Then, start putting the moves on her: play with her hair, touch her leg, and when the moment is right...lean in and give her a kiss. And I mean a real kiss with some tongue.

If she's into it, let your hands wander. Move to the car or a private booth and play with her nipples, grab her ass and rub on her pussy. But for now, don't go any further. Just enjoy the female form.

You'll have another opportunity later in the game to get real down and dirty...

Chapter 2: Virgin Territory

Ever wonder why so many movies and TV shows take place in high school? American Pie, Mean Girls, Gossip Girl...they're all about the chase!

These were the days when you were still holding on to (or attempting to hold on to) your virginity. You'd explore your sexuality for hours at a time without actually fucking – and that is a huge mental and physical turn on.

So, we're taking it back to the basics! Before you had sex and before you got married...you're now an innocent virgin and this chapter is just one big tease.

Some challenges will be a 1-woman show and some challenges will be shared with your Boy Toy of the week or any guy you start dating along the journey.

Have fun, you bad girl.

14. Study your Cookie with a Mirror

I need you to do something right now. Yes, as you're reading this. Put your hand down your pants. You feel that? That is your vulva.

Now, insert your fingers inside of yourself. Feel that? That's your vagina.

And together, your vulva and your vagina equal your "cookie." At least, that's what I call her.

It's time to get acquainted with your cookie. Grab a mirror or lay in front of a mirror on the floor. Take your panties off and spread your legs. Explore and play with yourself. Rub, finger, and just look at how sensual your cookie can be.

For most girls, they've never had such an up-close look. Sometimes it can be scary. Sometimes it can evoke a "That's what I look like!" reaction. And that's normal!

Vaginas, Vulvas and Clitorises literally come in all shapes and colors. Yours is perfect.

15. Get the Most Luxurious Vibrator Money Can Buy

Treat yourself, woman! After all you've been through this past year or so, you deserve some major stress relief, don't ya think?

Go for a vibrator with a curved shaft and a smaller tickler on the top. This takes care of both penetration and clitoral stimulation.

Google "The Rabbit Vibrator" and you'll see what I'm talking about...

16. Watch Porn and Touch Yourself

The two biggest bullshit statements of all time are "Girls don't want porn" and "Girls don't like porn". Bitch, please. Porn is amazing. Not only is porn a great teacher, but it also gives you a chance to learn what turns you on.

Fun fact: Most women get off to Lesbian Porn. It's just so hot.

17. Masturbate without Porn

Use that "Spank Bank" in your mind. You need to shuffle through your memories and fantasies from time to time as a self-exploration venture. When you've had the time to masturbate to sexual fantasies on your own, you can later draw on these fantasies when you man is going down on you. Knowing what turns you on is step 1 in owning your sexuality!

18. Dry Hump – xxx

Don't underestimate how hot and steamy this innocent little tease can be.

Get on top of your partner and start slowly kissing their neck and nibbling on their ear while you slowly begin to grind on their lap. This will progress into a full on make out session with a hard cock and wet panties.

The Rule: No sex and nothing beneath the clothes. You've got to walk away like a good little virgins.

19. Make Out Only

(Hands in Neutral Territory!)

xxx

Rediscover what it feels like to kiss someone with no end goal in sight. There is no rush to tear each other's clothes off or carry the situation to the bedroom.

Be a tease. Create that sexual tension. And walk away with never passing first base.

20. Make Out and Touch

(Over the Clothes Only!)

Kiss and let your hands play along. Let him grab you ass and feel you up. Rub on that hard bulge in his pants and let him rub you through your panties. And just like before...walk away before it escalates.

As the xxx rule dictates, you can only complete a second bucket list challenge after 1 hour.

21. Give Him a Hand Job

The key to a good hand job is lots of lube, whether that be KY Lube, Coconut Oil or spit and saliva – get that bad boy wet.
Ask your man to show you how he likes it OR tease him until he utterly cannot stand it anymore and is begging you to make him cum.

The Rules: You cannot use your mouth and he cannot finish himself.

22. Let Him Watch

Lay back and please yourself just like you would alone. Do whatever it is that turns you on and let him learn how you like to be touched and what brings you to orgasm.

23. Mutual Stimulation

The more turned on you are, the more love you put into that hand job. The hotter his hand job is, the more vigorously those fingers are going to finger your beautiful pussy. Don't put any pressure on each other to cum, just enjoy the ride and see where it takes you.

24. Titty Fuck

Let's assume that you and your victim are extra horny virgins with an imagination, shall we?

Let him slide his cock in-between those two beautiful breasts as he pleasures himself. The girl can rub her nipples at the same time to really get in the spirit.

This game isn't just for Double D's! If you don't have a tit valley to work with, a hand job while rubbing the tip of his penis all over your nipples will work, too.

And remember: lube is your friend.

25. Just the Tip

The most virgin move of all! When you really want to have sex but still want to be a good girl, did tip of his cock in "just to see how it feels." It doesn't count as sex if it's just the tip, right?

Chapter 3: Cyber Tease

Sex on a screen is all about imagination! Don't underestimate the power of some simple dirty talk, some naturally sexy moans, and a few naughty photos...

26. Sext

Now that you've got your target, warm them up with some friendly banter. You want to build the tension before you go in for the kill.

Start slow with something subtle to gauge the temperature in the room. Use lines like...

✓ **I had the hottest sex dream about you**
✓ **I been wondering what those big hands could do to my body... any ideas?**

Then work your way up to the dirty stuff like...

✓ I want you to slap my ass so hard that you live a bright red mark

✓ I would look soooo hot with your cock down my throat.

To put a naughty spin on this one, text your target mid-day when he's at work.

27. Tease Him with Sexy Photos

#SendNudes

Men are visual creatures. Send him a sexy photo of yourself in the gym locker room with those tight sport bra titties or a photo of you all wet right out of the shower. Or if you're new to this whole sexy selfie thing, put on a tank top, lay down in bed, and take a trillion photos with different faces and angles- then pick which is your favorite.

Remember, don't try too hard to be sexy! Just be natural. Natural is sexy.

Pro Tip: Only send these photos to a guy that you trust. If he hasn't totally won your trust yet, **don't include your face** in the racy photos.

28. SnapChat Sex

If you are new to the digital era, let me tell you that SnapChat is so much fun! It's basically an app where you can take photos or videos with cute filters and send the photos to friends. Once the photo is "opened", it disappears after a few seconds.

This is the perfect tease for your target AND it lets you keep your dignity in a new relationship.

Start innocent with a sexy photo showing some cleavage or you in your bra. Then work your way up to a clip of you playing with yourself. If you want to be really naughty...send a series of clips until you cum on camera. This will drive him crazy.

Ps. The way to add guys on SnapChat is to ask for their User Name first.

29. Cyber Sex

When you're at home in bed, Facetime or Skype your crush wearing a super low cut top. On the bottom, you should be wearing something with easy access- either just panties or a negligee dress.

Give him a little tease, ask him what he would do to you if he was in bed with you. As you start talking dirty, let your hands wander your body. Start playing with yourself to really get in the mood. Once you ask to see his hard cock- it's game on.

Clothes may be shed, toys may be used, and full on orgasms may be had.

30. Booty Call

You want sex and nothing else. No dinner, no cuddling, and no sleepovers. You literally call the shots on this one.

Text him with a demand for sex and a time frame. Like this...

"I have 1 hour and I'm super horny. Come over and fuck me".

He'll leave thinking, "What the hell just happened" and this imbalance of perceived power will rock his world.

Chapter 4: Everything Oral

What is the first sexual pleasure to disappear in a marriage? That tongue action, of course.

But when you have a brand-new boy in front of you...one that you can't keep your hands off of...you suddenly find a dick in your mouth 8 days a week.

As for your cookie, it's time to share that sweetness with a man that loves to please!

Oh, and have I mentioned that eating ass has become really popular in the past couple years? There's certainly something you've been missing while you were married...

So here's to spicing up your oral game with some fun challenges for your tongue and his!

31. Get a Brazilian Wax

Men are visual creatures. Give him a full view of that beautiful cookie with a Brazilian Wax! This wax treatment removes every hair in sight, including the inside of your butt cheeks!

Some things to know about a Brazilian Wax:

- **Yes, it stings**
- **No, you won't die.**
- **The waxing specialist will spread you open and really get in there.**
- **Your vagina doesn't look weird. The specialist has seen every kind of cookie under the sun.**

- Waxes usually last 3 weeks before hair grows back
- The more often you wax, the less it hurts as the hair thins out AND the slower it grows back.

32. TELL Him to Go Down on You

Why are us women afraid to ask for what we want? Have you ever met a man who was too shy to ask for a blow job? HELL NO.

Now that you're entering a new phase of sexual power, it's time to take control. As soon as things start heating up and clothes start coming off - just **tell him**, "Go down on me."

Don't hesitate to tell him how you like it, too.

Use commands!

- ✓ **Lower**
- ✓ **A little Faster**
- ✓ **No fingers**

Or do what I do when a guy isn't exactly licking the right spot...guide his head to exactly where you like it. Girls are like a Rubik's Cube; each one with a different combination!

And hey, no pressure. You don't have to cum. In fact, if he's a stranger, you might *not* cum and that's okay. This Bucket List Challenge is about learning to <u>ask</u> for what feels good.

33. Give the Best Blow Job Ever

Cumming from oral and cumming from sex are 2 totally different experiences. Treat him to a relaxing and sensual BJ however you like it. Play with that cock in new ways. Lick it, spit on it, slap it against your tongue, rub it on your lips. Really make this blowie your own.

34. Blow Job Under the Table

While he's having his morning coffee at the table or in the middle of dinner at the kitchen table, gracefully slide under the table and unzip his pants. The rest is up to you and your mouth. Enjoy yourself down there.

35. Sweet Cunnilingus

Chocolate Syrup, Ice Cream, Frosting – it's time for dessert.

Here's the challenge: absolutely cover your pretty pussy in the tasty treat of your choice.

He's going to lick all of it up until you cum. Don't be afraid to make a mess. The best oral is always messy.

36. The Lollipop Blow Job

Ready to get messy?

Before you start sucking on him, start sucking on a lollipop while you get him started with your other hand. Watching you lick your lollipop will get him instantly hard.

After you've teased him enough, use all of that extra saliva and sticky juice in your mouth to give him the tastiest blow job ever – just don't put that lollipop down. Stop once in a while to suck a little more, spit some of those juices all over his cock, and tease him while he begs for you to finish.

37. Have him Eat your Ass

It's the dawn of a new era in oral sex. The asshole shall never be neglected again! Girls, if you've ever had your ass licked, holy hell you are in for a treat. As for the guys...they've have been wanting to do this for a while, trust me.

Don't know how to ask for it? Just tell him, "You know what really turns me on...? I love when a guy plays with my ass." Once he starts rubbing it, you can simply tell him, "Use your tongue" and watch how fast he turns you over!

38. Sixty-Nine

Him lying on his back, you straddling his face while his cock is perfectly positioned to play with- this mutual pleasure is the underrated sex position: 69.

Ladies, you can use your hands and your mouth here. Guys, can use their hands to move you back and fourth on their face for some extra stimulation.

39. Give Him Head While Playing with a Vibrator

You'll hear this statement over and over throughout this Bucket List... "The more pleasure you get-the more pleasure you give."

Turn yourself on the next time you're giving head with a little toy of your own. Use your vibrator to penetrate you or stimulate your clit while you're sucking away. This will be an amazing (and very likely, orgasmic) experience for the both of you.

40. Swallow

For a man, having the tip of his penis licked and sucked from the very beginning to the very end of a blow job is absolutely mind-blowing. Be a good girl and let him finish in your mouth.

Pro Tip: To make this even hotter, make eye contact while he's cumming.

41. Ride His Face

There are two super sexy ways to ride your man's tongue.

One: Sit on his face and smother him with your pretty pussy. He'll love it. Don't be afraid to gently ride him with a back and forth motion, giving his tongue a little bit of encouragement. Better yet, have something sturdy to hold onto. This will allow you to relax and enjoy.

Two Have him get on his knees while you put one leg up on the kitchen counter or desk. This will give him full access to all the fun areas. He can also use his hands to move your body against his tongue.

42. Play with his Balls

The balls get neglected, mainly because us women aren't taught what to do with them. The man should be vocal in what he likes. Licking? Sucking? Cupping? Ask him.

And don't forget to pay attention to his perineum — the nerve-packed area of skin between his balls and his butt.

You can lick as his assistant while he pleasures himself or take little detours while giving him head.

Chapter 5: Sex Sex Sex

This chapter is all about breaking your sexual routine. We all get into a sexual routine, especially when we've have the same partner for such a long time. Usually it's missionary to doggy and then we're done.

Not anymore.

Say "Goodbye" to choreographed sex and hello to ALL of the positions in ALL of the places. Not only will these sexy ideas switch up your sex routine, but also, the adrenaline and sensation of new angles make each sexual experience feel like it's your first time.

Have at it...

43. Have Sex with Another Girl

It's crossed your mind, hasn't it?

While you're on this whole journey of sexual rediscovery, why not go for it?! Girl on girl is one of the ultimate Bucket List fantasies for us females. Women are so sensual, so pretty, and so sexy to play with!

Whether you hook up with an acquaintance who you find attractive after a couple of Tequila shots or a girl who you matched with on Tinder, give her pussy a taste.

44. Have a One-Night Stand

Take a dude home from the bar and never speak to him again.

Or at least, don't have the intention of ever speaking to him again (if fate wants you to see him again, you will).

45. The Reverse One-Night Stand

Okay, it's time to learn the tricks of the trade when it comes to dating like a boss.

Did you go home with a guy that you really want to see again? You're going to have to sacrifice a piece of clothing or jewelry to ensure that you'll see him.

Immature? Maybe. Effective? Definitely.

Leave something at his place. Just make sure you have a way to contact him later so that you can make a time to meet up to "get your sweater back".

46. Missionary with Pillow Assistance

The most underrated sexual position in history is missionary! Missionary lets you be close to your man as he fucks you hard or makes love to you gently (yes, that's a thing). You can watch him penetrate you while he watches the look of pleasure on your face.

If you've ever had sex, you'd had missionary. But have you ever had missionary with a pillow as a prop?

Slide a pillow under your hips. This raises you up and gives your man the ability to get even deeper with each thrust!

47.Missionary & Clitoral Stimulation

This one sounds like the title of a Broadway play...and trust me, it will be just as dramatic.

While your man slowly penetrates you, start rubbing your clit. As you keep going and get close to orgasm, your juices will drench his cock. When your just about to cum, he'll be able to feel you contracting all around him- pushing him even further over the edge.

Pro Tip: If you're like most girls and can't come with the snap of a finger, try rubbing your clit with your eyes closed – just like you would when you're masturbating.

If this feels awkward to you, say, "Hey, I'm going to masturbate, and I want you to fuck me while I do." This initiates that it's all about you and you don't give a shit if he cums (even though he 100% will).

48. Spice Up Doggy Style

Because you're a bad bitch who likes to be in control, try Doggy Style your way.

Tell your man to stay still as you back up on that cock. Use your own rhythm, fast or slow, as so that you can feel every inch of him going inside and out. He will absolutely melt with this new sensation.

And since you're in control, give him some commands: slap my ass, pull my hair, and (best of all) rub on my asshole with some spit.

You've got access to lots of stimulating activities back there.

49. Restrained Doggy

No actual leashes here, but in this position, your guy has full control over you by grabbing both of your arms and holding them behind your back. This gives you the feeling of total helplessness and the flexibility factor allows you both to hit a spot that you may have never hit before.

50. Sex with the Lights On

It's a little weird at first. Every woman who has watched her naked body bounce up and down goes through the internal questionnaire. Do I look okay from this angle? Is my pussy pretty? Am I supposed to look him in the eyes?

This is normal!

Not only will you get used to this, but you'll start to like it. Watch him penetrate you and watch his eyes roll back in his head while you ride him.

Ps. Guys are visual creatures, so to answer your question: **Yes,** you look hot from every angle.

51. Sex Right after You Cum

Whether you cum from oral, clitoral stimulation, masturbation or straight up penetration- the sensation of being fucked while you've just cum is insane. Often, a guy sticking his hard cock in you while you're still orgasming can provide either an elongated orgasm or multiple orgasms.

52. Cowgirl

Ladies on top. Hold on to the headboard or put your hands on his chest as you ride him.

While you're up there, try the Froggy variation of Cowgirl as you put your feet flat on the mattress or floor. Now you can do mini squats up and down on his hard cock. This position is fantastic for hitting your g-spot.

53. Still Cowgirl

Just like it sounds! Climb on top but don't move. Instead, your man will hold your hips and thrust in and out as you enjoy being pounded from below.

54. Reverse Cowgirl

This one takes some practice (and some balance).

Reverse cowgirl is when you're on top, but facing away from the dude. Sometimes this position can be tricky when it comes to moving your hips up and down. To get some more friction, lean forward and put your hands between his legs for leverage. Alternatively, let your man try pumping up into you (like he's definitely seen in the pornos).

55. Pole Position

This position provides double stimulation for girls as you grind your clit against his leg while also being penetrated.

He'll lie on his back with one leg bent, foot flat on the ground. You'll sit on him, reverse cowgirl style, with his perched leg in-between your legs. Then using his knee for balance, bounce on his hard dick while rubbing yourself to orgasm on his leg.

56. Let him Cum Wherever He Wants

Tits, ass, stomach, face... get creative. Just when he is about to blow, ask him where he wants to cum (it doesn't always have to be your mouth!)

57. Sex in Front of a Mirror

Find the room in your house with the biggest mirror and give yourselves a sex show!

Bend yourself over the bathroom counter and watch him hit it from the back. Have sex on the floor in front of your closet door mirrors. Or go all out and have a mirror installed above your bed.

Adding this element of visualization to the mix intensifies the entire experience.

Don't like the way you look in that angle? Move. Laugh. Have fun. You don't have to be a porn star here.

58. Use Lots of Lube

Sex with proper lube is a mind-blowing experience. Everything is more sensitive and you're able to try a lot of tight positions that may not have worked before. Many studies have shown that using lube can help increase the likelihood of having an orgasm by 50%. Those odds are just too good not to try!

You can buy KY lube or use coconut oil, both of which are long lasting forms of lube, rather than just using spit or relying on natural body lubrication.

59. Spooning

This is one of those positions where lube makes a world of difference! Get into the spooning position. Your man will slide his hard cock between your legs for the perfect angle of penetration. He can hold your waist or legs for extra leverage.

Pro Tip: Try wrapping one of your legs over his legs for extra deep access.

60. Sex on the Floor

While a mattress has a bit of bounce that moves with you, the floor give you total control during sex and allows you to get a bit deeper.

The floor is particularly fantastic for any kind of cowgirl position!

61. Spankings

The science behind spanking is this: those little bursts of pain release feel-good hormones into your body, creating a euphonic rush.

Also, it's fun to be treated like a bad girl from time to time.

Maybe you want them lightly or maybe you want your ass to be full of red handprints.

You can use your hand, a paddle, a belt, a wooden spoon...get creative and don't be afraid to check out some toys on Amazon.

62. Have your Hair Pulled

There is a proper and improper way to pull a woman's hair.

Improper: Grabbing her hair by the loose ends or the end of a ponytail. This yanking causes whiplash. There's nothing sexy about that.

Proper: Grabbing a handful of hair by the root and holding it in place. The pulling comes along naturally as your bodies move together.

When you want it, tell him and teach him. Don't be afraid to speak up. Odds are, he wants to be a little rough with you but isn't sure if he's allowed.

63. Get Choked

Getting choked during sex is so hot. Restricting just the right amount of air to your brain creates a euphoric sensation all over your body! For many girls, choking enhances the feeling of penetration.

Not too hard, not too soft and not for too long. When it comes to choking during sex, start out with 10 seconds at a time. You don't want to pass out.

Remember: The goal is to lightly target the airway, not your vocal box. Guide him to avoid squeezing the very center of your throat. Choke yourself next time you masturbate to see what and where you like it.

64. Rough Sex

I mean...really rough.

Once you have established how much hair pulling you like, how much choking you can handle, and how hard you like your ass slapped, go all out. Bite, bruise, and leave a mark!

Push him up against the wall, let him throw you on the bed...and if you like, add light slapping and dirty talk in the mix, you little slut.

65. Sex on the Stairs

The angles you can get on the stairs are magical! Doggy, cowgirl, acrobatic bending and twisting. Just be sure to get busy at the bottom of the stairs. Safety first!

66. The Sleeper

Lay on your stomach with your legs together like you're sunbathing. Your man, using lots of lube for help, slides his cock between your legs, entering you as he pushes between your thighs.

That extra friction adds even more sensation for him and the angle of this position will hit a new spot for you.

67. Legs Up

To get the deepest possible penetration, lay on your back and put your ankles on his shoulders while he pounds you.

For an even more intense variation to this position, have your man grab both of your ankles and puts them both on one shoulder as he wraps one arm around both legs, pulling you deeper and deeper.

68. Sex in the Shower

Start by soaping each other up – a luffa is a worthy investment for this dirty play spot. Let him rub soap all over your beautiful breasts and massage bath gel all over his sexy chest.

When it comes time for full on sex, try a version of doggy where you use the wall as support. Another slip-proof shower position is where your man sits on the shower floor while you ride him -using his shoulders for leverage.

69. Sex in a Hotel

The fancier, the better! There's nothing like having a night of hot sex and room service in a comfy hotel room with fluffy pillows and soft bath robes. Once that door is closed, it's like time stops and there's nothing but you and the man you're undressing.

To pull this one off, you have 2 options:

1. Hang out in the bar at a fancy hotel lobby. You can bring a girlfriend for

with the same goal of hooking up with a businessman traveling on his work credit card. If he asks what you're doing hanging out at a hotel lobby bar, just say they make the best mojitos in town!

2. Get on Tinder and look for someone in town for the weekend. Make sure you have a good repertoire before you go to his hotel room for safety AND to ensure he's going to show you a good time.

70.Sex in the Car

Park somewhere secluded and quiet - just like back in high school. Get in the back seat and see how many positions you can come up with as you bend and contort your body.

If you don't feel comfortable doing this in public, climb on top of him once he parks the car in the garage.

Pro Tip: Just don't turn the car on with the garage door down; trapped fumes are very dangerous! You can't have sex if you're both unconscious...

71. Sexy Oil Massage

Not only do you get a full-body rub down with oils and lotions of your choosing, but this massage will inadvertently turn into sex. So, you also get manual stimulation and full penetration while you don't have to lift a finger.

72. Middle of the Night Sex

The next time you have a man in your bed, take advantage of every moment. When you stir in the middle of the night or get up to use the restroom, use that as an opportunity to have blissful half-awake sex. Your barely coherent state of mind makes for some seriously hot carnal sex.

Slowly start touching him and kissing him until he's half awake. If he still doesn't get the picture, climb on top of him.

When you're done, fall back asleep and anticipate waking up in a wonderful mood.

73. Morning Sex

Why waste that morning wood?

Both men and women have high levels of sex hormones in the morning, perfect for fueling an intense sex session.

When you haven't brushed your teeth yet, just slowly start grinding on him in the spooning position. As you feel that hard cock on your ass, you'll start to get wetter and wetter until he can easily slide into you from behind.

Pro Tip: Morning sex is great for hangovers and is the antidote to awkward morning wake ups with a stranger.

74. Do the Walk of Shame

Which brings us to our next point! It happens to the best of us. Drag your cute ass out of bed at 8am, dress and heels on from the night before, and schlep yourself across town while still a little tipsy.

Be proud of what you have conquered, my queen!

75. Have a Threesome

This is called a Bucket List for a reason! A threesome is the ultimate sexual fantasy that every bad girl should cross off her list!

Here are your options to easily slide into a threesome...

➢ Get on Tinder and look for a couple seeking a girl to play with.

➢ Go out to a bar with the idea of going home with a couple. Start flirting with the girl, first. If she's into it, the guy will follow.

➢ Talk to a naughty girlfriend of yours about this bucket list, and see if she'd want to join you in seducing a man (or another woman)

Watch some threesome pornos to see what you like. And be safe! If you've found a couple online, meet them at a bar first to make sure you get a good vibe.

76. A Quickie

Mastering the art of quickies is key to a healthy sex life.

Get those endorphins pumping and those serotonin levels flowing with a quick five to ten-minute bang.

Message that guy you've been seeing and tell him to meet you at your house at lunch. Grab your hot coworker and bang in the bathroom. Pause the movie, fuck his brains out, and then press play with an invigorated attention span.

The only rule to quickies: Don't settle for a quickie when you have time for a full sex session!

Chapter 6: Boyfriends Only

Dating isn't what it used to be.

With all of these online dating apps, some boyfriends last for a week, some last for a couple of months, and some last for well into your future.

Regardless of his exact shelf life, save special challenges for the guys who have earned the messy stuff, the vulnerable stuff, and the stuff that requires some trust and practice.

77. Buy Some Sexy Lingerie

...and wear it to dinner.

Weather it's some sexy thigh-high stockings under your skirt or a sheer body suit under your jeans and top...don't show him until he starts to undress you once you get home.

You'll feel sexy the whole night knowing that you have a secret. And he'll always be on his toes wondering, "What's she got under there tonight?"

78. Phone Sex

Anywhere, any time- the element of surprise and the use of spontaneity is so hot. Call your man while he's at work, or lounging at home. Catching him off-guard adds thrill to the fire.

Don't text him to say you're going to call. Just call him.

When he answers, tell him that you're super horny. Talk about how you're touching yourself thinking about what you want to do to him. And then ask him what he wants to do to you. Tell him that you can't stop thinking about the sex you had the other night, or that you are so wet just thinking about his hard cock.

He'll be dying to get his hands on you.

79. Have him Go Down on You Until you Cum

You cannot cross this one off the list until you cum!

Eating a woman's pussy is like an Olympic sport. Each sport takes practice and dedication. To make a woman cum via tongue takes the right amount of pressure, speed, and time. Every woman is different so help him out and tell him what you like! Lower, softer, faster, no fingers...speak up, woman!

He is your tool. Think of something sexy, lay back, and know that he's not going to stop licking until your body shakes and you cum all over his face.

80. Period Sex

Throw a towel down on the bed and go to town. The extra lubrication provides a whole new sensation and the blood puts you into a state of "Is this real life"? Not to mention, the act of sex during a girl's period can help decrease the pain of cramps.

Ps. You *can* get pregnant while on your period. Still use protection.

81. Butt Plug for You

While the name doesn't sound very glamorous, you can actually find some sexy looking butt plugs made of shiny silicone, rubber, or harder plastics – some even with jewels on the end or with a sparkly finish.

With a rounded-cone like shape and a large handle/stopper, butt plugs are to be inserted into your ass to stimulate your g-spot.

You can keep the butt plug in for foreplay, sex or just testing your limits on your own. This creates the feeling of being totally filled up, awakening all of your erogenous zones down there. Or your partner can tease you and fuck you with just the plug.

Before you even try anal, play around with this toy. You've got to walk before you can run, girl.

82. Anal Penetration

Anal is something that takes a lot of care and practice. Many girls who LOVE anal report that it took the 2-3 times to enjoy it, but they were committed to the cause because mentally, they liked the idea.

Have your man start out with his fingers and lots of lube, gently rubbing and inserting his fingers as you relax. When your ass is ready, have your man slowly put in just the tip. Relax. Go slow. Very slow. Don't be a hero.

83. Play with His Ass

Yes, I said it! HIS ass. While you're giving him a blow job, get your finger wet and rub it on his ass. If you're comfortable, let your tongue graze over his asshole a few times. Getting to this level of comfort together will be a sexual bonding experience he'll never forget.

84. Put a Finger In

Your finger. His ass. Yep, we're not done with the ass play yet.

After you've licked and rubbed on it a few times during sex, you'll both be comfortable in that region. So now, it's time to explore a little deeper.

Each man has a G-spot located inside of his ass. Researchers have described this G-spot as basically male clitoris packed with nerve endings that can give him a full-body orgasm. To do this, stick your finger inside and find his prostate (aka G-spot). You're looking for a grape-sized ball about three-quarters of a finger length inside him bum. One finger and a "come hither" motion will do the trick. Rub on it just as he's about to cum!

Pro Tip: With any asshole, lube is your friend. Use proper KY Lube or Coconut Oil to do the trick.

85. Rough Blow Job

In a forced blow job, the man has all the power. You can make this as gentle or aggressive as you like- just tell him what you want beforehand.

Explain to him that you have this fantasy where he grabs you by the back of her hair and guides your mouth up and down his cock. For you naughty girls, tell him push your head deep down onto his cock until it reaches that back of your throat. If you've never gagged on your man's dick before, you're missing out.

86. Role Play

We all have a fantasy, but not all of us are comfortable acting it out. But remember, students, this is your Sex Ed assignment. It's mandatory!

In each role play scenario, you can decide who plays who. There are no gender norms in fantasy land. The only rule, stick with each role play for at least 20 minutes; sometimes it takes a while for the imagination to warm up. And if you're having a pleasurable time...keep going.

To start out, pick one of the 3 role plays, set your alarm for 20 minutes and get into it...for science.

Escort / Client: You're his call girl that he's paying for dirty sex. You have to do anything and everything that he says once you show up at his hotel door.

Doctor/Patient: You're not feeling well. The doctor has to find where it hurts and make it better by any means necessary.

Teacher / Bad Student: You didn't turn in your homework...again! Instead, you've been a bad little slut who hasn't been paying attention to her studies. Now, you must be punished.

87. Go to a Strip Club Together

Just the two of you - this is going to be the kinkiest date you've ever had. Maybe you'll watch him get turned on and you'll get a little hot and bothered yourself. Or maybe the two of you will feel incredibly awkward and giggle your whole way through.

No matter what, the sexual tension afterwards will be lingering. Sit in the car and touch each other before you leave the parking lot.

88. Go to a Sex Club Together

Sex Club, Swingers Club, Kink Club...whatever you can find in your area. These clubs are for... Exhibitionists: People who like to have sex in front of other people.

102

Swingers: Couples that like to swap and share partners with other couples.

Voyeurs: Those who just like to watch.

Curious Folk: People who are new to the concept of sex clubs and just want to check it out.

Everyone is welcome in a sex club! No one will push you and your boo to do anything you don't want to do. You won't be pressured to get involved. And you won't be the only first timers.

You and your boyfriend will either leave laughing your heads off together or totally turned on with the idea of getting involved.

Baby steps are okay here!

Chapter 7: Playing in Public

Third date? You officially have the green light to get a little naughty!

That feeling of doing something dirty at the risk of getting caught can be such a turn on. The delayed gratification of slow foreplay and the build up to hot and heavy sex is something that bonds two people together like no other.

89. Sext at Dinner

Go to a nice restaurant. One where you should be on your best, if not decent, behavior. Start with a couple dirty texts at the table. Tell him what you want to do his body and watch him squirm with excitement.

Then after you've got him all hot and bothered, get up and go to the bathroom where you'll send him a dirty selfie. It can be a photo of you touching yourself, of your panties, of the lingerie you're wearing underneath...something that will drive him crazy. which must be opened discretely at the table. Come back to the table like nothing happened...

90. At the Movie Theatre

It's dark, it's loud and it's the perfect place to do everything and anything to each other's' bodies. Hand jobs and pussy rubbing are an easy escapade to accomplish in a crowded theatre. You can reach over for a little tug action or lay your legs across his lap, giving him full access.

Oh and that popcorn you dropped down your shirt? You're going to need some help getting that out.

Pro Tip: Go to a movie that's been out for weeks and you're more likely to get a bit of privacy.

91. Remote Control Bullet Vibrator

Vibrator bullets fit perfectly up your pussy, while your man holds the remote control. He can increase the vibrators speed and change up the settings whenever and wherever he likes.

Before dinner or a party, slip the vibrator in your pussy and hand him the controls. The vibrator is small enough that you may even forget that it's inside of you...at least until he turns it on while the waiter is taking your order.

92. Get Fingered in the Car

To get ready for this dirty escapade, wear a skirt or a dress; something with easy access. Grab his hand and show him exactly where to put it. Have him start by rubbing over your panties. Then either slide your panties to the side, or take them off while he's driving. Then, when you're super wet, have him slide his fingers inside of you.

Pro Tip: If you don't have tinted windows, you'll have to be sneaky about this one.

93. Road Head

Driving on the back roads or driving at night is the perfect time to unzip his pants and have a little fun on the drive home. Make sure he keeps his eyes on the road, otherwise he may have to pull over if he gets really into it.

94. Sex in a Public Restroom

At the bar and just need to jump his bones right away? Use the bathroom! Whisper in his ear, "Meet me in the bathroom in 30 seconds".

You'll get up first to secure the spot. He'll follow quickly behind. You'll already have your panties slid to the side while playing with yourself. Have him slide inside of you either sitting on the counter or bent over with hands on the wall. He may have to cover your mouth to stop the moans.

When you leave, do it like nothing ever happened and no one will suspect a thing.

Pro Tip: If you're out to dinner, have hot bathroom sex after you've paid your bill. Your waiter won't be looking for you and you can make a sneaky exit once you've finished.

Chapter 8: Sex Games

Sex doesn't always have to be serious. Sex can be fun, too. In fact, laughter and a sense of play helps break the tension during new sexual experiences. Playing games and goofing around will bring you both out of your shell, allowing you to try new things and push each other's' erotic boundaries comfortably.

Here are a few games to play with the boy who's sexy and fun...

95. Porn Night

What a fun date idea, right?

Take turns picking a porn- it doesn't matter the category. Start out with some categories neither of you watch on your own like MILF porn or Bondage to warm up- these are categories that you can both giggle about together and maybe get some new ideas. Go in with the mindset that this is going to be an entertaining activity together...while we all know that it's impossible not to get turned on.

Eventually, start showing each other what you like to watch...and see how long you can go without turning the night into your own porno.

96. No Moving Allowed

We want to cum! Usually, when someone is giving us oral, we are trying to make ourselves cum. But the orgasms are so much stronger when you just let them happen.

So here's the rule: While you go down on your man, they aren't allowed to move. Not their hands or their hips. Every time they move, you stop sucking or licking. They will be forced to lay back and let that orgasm take over their entire body.

This is the hottest blowjob he's ever gotten and you best believe, he'll be replaying this sexual encounter over and over again in his head until the end of time.

97. Sex Dice

Your sexual experience is all up to fate with a roll of the dice.

So, there are two dice: one dice lists different activities like "lick", "tickle", "squeeze" and the other dice lists body parts like "nipples", "ass", "belly button".

This is a fun game to play with a glass of wine on the floor and see where it leads.

98. The 10-Minute Rule

The dominant person in this scenario sets a timer for 10 minutes. In those ten minutes, they tease their submissive partner relentlessly- nothing is off limits. The catch? The submissive partner is not allowed to touch the dominant partner until the timer goes off. But watch out, that timer will release a ravenous beast.

99. Strip Poker

Or Strip Chess. Or Strip Checkers. Or Strip Battle Ship. You can turn any game into a stripping game if you just believe in yourselves.

This kind of playful spirit brings out the flirt in both of you. The tease of watching clothes slowly coming off is wonderfully torturous. And that competitive edge will add a little spice to the dynamic.

If you want to step the game up one more level, you can make a rule that whoever is naked first receives a penalty of performing some slutty sex act or spankings

100.Netflix & Chill

Now, for the last bucket list challenge... you get to see what this whole "Netflix and Chill" thing really means!

Say you're talking to a guy for a while and you really just want to fuck him, but play hard to get at the same time...invite him over "to watch Netflix".

Put on your cutest 'lounging around the house' outfit – maybe some booty shorts and a cozy t-shirt with a sexy bra underneath. Invite him over, get cozy on the couch, and put on a movie. Cuddle. Touch. Kiss. Odds are, you won't finish the movie...but it wasn't important anyways.

Finished the Challenge?

You dirty girl...

But hey, you're not done yet.

Now you need to scan through the past 100 sexual experiences and pick your top 5s.

Which naughty acts did you play over and over again in your head? Which one made you cum the hardest? Which one do you want to try again until you can perfect it?

You've learned some important lessons. Write them down.

On the other hand, which Bucket List Challenges weren't for you? Did you not like getting choked? Was fucking a girl just not for you? Know your boundaries and stick to them.

The is the beginning of your new chapter. Live you life by your rules and find a man that fits the new you, in every sense of the word...

Top 5 Favorite Sex Challenges

1. _____

2. _____

3. _____

4. _____

5. _____

Top 5 Least Favorite Sex Challenges

1. _____

2. _____

3. _____

4. _____

5. _____

Your New Naughty Challenge?

To explore the sexual experiences above, weaving them into your normal sex life...that is, if you can consider your sex life "normal" anymore.

By now, you've gained a renewed sense of YOU. You are not the same woman that got married and you are not the same woman who got divorced. You are the new you. The new you is a confident queen who knows what she likes and what she needs...and she isn't afraid to ask for it.

Whether you realize it now, or you look back in 5 years and realize it then – you, my pretty princess, are a changed woman.

You are officially sexually awakened and sexually empowered. You walk with radiating self-worth, you eye-fuck a guy with confidence, and you take your clothes off only for the men who are worth your damn time.

You've conquered each challenge and you've grown with each experienced.

You are the fiercest you've ever been.
Don't let that go.

Sex Facts for Thought

➤ Men reach their sexual peak in their early 20's. Women reach their sexual peak in their mid-30's. In other words, our bodies and brains are best programed for wild, nasty sex at these ages. You are closer to your prime and peak now, than you were when you got married.

➤ Only around 25-30% of Women can orgasm from just penetration. That means almost 70% of women need clitoral stimulation to reach orgasm.

➤ The clitoral orgasm and the vaginal orgasm are different! These orgasms occur using different muscles in and nerve endings in your cookie area, and therefore feel different- and for some women, they don't even feel related. If you've only had a clitoral orgasm and want to feel a vaginal orgasm, try penetrating yourself with a vibrator (or your man) while you make yourself cum. Just the addition of simultaneous vaginal stimulation will give you a new kind of orgasm.

➤ Simultaneous Orgasms are Rare. Pornos may have you believing that couples often cum at the same time, but this is actually not how it works in real life. Men come easier and more often than the woman, that why we've got to speak up.

➤ Men have a G-spot, that super erogenous zone located right inside of his asshole. When stimulated by massaging or penetration, can provide euphoric sensations.

➤ Studies have shown that having sex with socks on increases the likelihood of an orgasm by 13-30%.

➤ Sex can make you better when you're sick. Sexual arousal and orgasm are shown to boost your immune system and put your recuperation into turbo mode.

➤ Amazon is a kinky lover's dream come true for discretely ordering lube, bondage gear, toys, and more.

➤ Sex is good for you! When you have sex, especially with your partner, your body releases endorphins, adrenaline, serotonin, and promotes healthy circulation. These benefits lead to less stress, healthier hearts, and decrease depression. Hello, good grades.

➤ There are 36 calories in the average male ejaculation. Mmm protein.

➤ According to Porn Hub data, Utah is the kinkiest state in terms of the taboo stuff that residents like to watch. But that's not really hard to believe, is it?

➤ Hookups can lead to marriage...if you can get past that first night of awkward sex. Actually, data shows that 1/3 of modern-day married couples started as a hookup.

> The Plan B Pill can be taken with 72 hours of unprotected sex and is sold at almost every pharmacy in the US for around $30. I'm just sayin'...it happens.

> The most effective birth control on the market is the Copper IUD Coil.

> "Medical Tourism" is a thing. Don't have health insurance and are hesitant to pay $1,000 for an IUD in the US? Plan a trip to Thailand (a country with one of the best healthcare standards in the world) where you can get an IUD for as low as $250...plus a vacation on the beach.

Have any questions? Need some advice? I'm no doctor, but I'm a responsible slut with all of the sexual wisdom.

Shoot me an email at
Alexa@TheTravelingBucketList.com

Anything you need will be our little secret...

Made in the USA
Columbia, SC
17 May 2019